More
Glasgow
by Tram

Ian G. McM. Stewart

PUBLISHED BY
THE
SCOTTISH TRAMWAY MUSEUM SOCIETY

95p

Frontispiece: This city scene at the Renfield Street junction with Sauchiehall Street illustrates admirably the impact of the trams on city life. They were everywhere. In this photograph alone there are four threading their predetermined paths through Glasgow's death-defying pedestrians. At least **they** haven't changed . . .

Cover: Sauchiehall Street from Hope Street corner in 1949, with three oft-recalled city "institutions" — Craig's Rhul tearooms and Copland's and Pettigrew's department stores — being passed by a fourth — the omnipresent tramcar.

First published September 1978.

By the same author: "Glasgow by Tram"; published 1977.

Printed by Crown Press (Keighley) Limited, Chapel Lane, Keighley, West Yorkshire

INTRODUCTION

It was not long after "Glasgow by Tram" was published before people were asking when the next in the series would be produced. So, one has a degree of sympathy for Richmal Crompton who produced over twenty-five "Just William" books and yet managed to vary the title for each. Here we are at only edition No. 2 and struggling for an appropriate title. It should of course convey what is inside: MORE GLASGOW BY TRAM.

The selection of photographs has been made so much easier by kind Glaswegians (some exiled) who have sent in their collections of album pictures or old commercial postcards. Some of these are quite valuable and certainly irreplaceable. One gentleman came all the way from Reading to hand his over lest the Post Office might mislay them. Much of his material has been reproduced. All the photographs emphasise the impact, indeed dominance of the faithful tramcar on the Greater Glasgow environment; always there or thereabouts.

An attempt has been made to reinforce coverage of areas shown in "Glasgow by Tram" which proved particularly popular — like the West End and also to illustrate areas which were not shown before. The terms of reference are unchanged: show Glasgow by, with or from and in the era of the tramcar. There are, as can be seen, still gaps. For instance, few photographers appear to have been out and about in Gorbals or Saltmarket. It may be that you can help fill such gaps. Who knows, if enough material amasses there may have to be a further edition and what will its title be? Write to the author at 9 Blackhouse Gardens, Newton Mearns, Glasgow, G77 5HS, and anything sent will be returned safely after copying.

In all this it is quite clear that folk are reluctant to see the past continuing to be destroyed. Almost too late, demolition and concrete are giving way to conservation and sand-blasted stonework.

Nostalgia lives!

IAN G. McM. STEWART,
M.C.I.B.S., M.I.Hosp.E.

ACKNOWLEDGEMENTS

The author wishes to thank the following for their assistance in preparing this book.

T. & R. Annan & Sons Ltd

Ian M. Coonie

Ian L. Cormack, M.A.

Brian T. Deans, B.A., M.Sc.

Gavin Drummond, A.C.I.S.

Chris K. Fletcher, R.I.B.A., A.R.I.A.S.

Hamilton Photography Ltd

Paul Hewett, F.I.E.D.

George Lane

Stuart M. Little, M.C.I.T.

Brian M. Longworth

Alistair A. Taylor, A.R.I.B.A., A.R.I.A.S.

Bill Tuckwell

Overleaf: Part of a map of Tramways in the Greater Glasgow area made by John Bartholomew and Sons Ltd in 1907. The scale as reproduced is approximately $\frac{1}{2}'' = 1$ mile.

MAP OF TRAMWAY SYSTEMS IN GLASGOW AND NEIGHBOURHOOD

Glasgow Corporation Tramways in operation
,, ,, ,, authorised and suggested extensions
Other Tramways in operation
Other Tramways authorised

TRONGATE

An early 1880s view of Trongate in the horse tramway period. The Tolbooth is on the right with the Tontine Hotel opposite the Tron Steeple. The lack of crowds would suggest that this was a Sunday.

The Tron Steeple photographed from Glasgow Cross before the Great War with green, red, blue and white trams in evidence. Only the yellow trams did not run along Argyle Street and Trongate and so the colour of the shops was well matched by those of the standard trams taking the crown of the road.

GEORGE SQUARE

This 1902 scene shows the north-west corner of George Square featuring the now-concealed Queen Street Station arch. The less said about the North British Railway's station nameboard the better. Perhaps this is where the money ran out.

This is the south west corner of the Square showing a Blairdardie tram which dates the picture. The extension to Blairdardie was opened in 1949 and there is no hint of trolleybus wires which began to adorn the south side of George Square for the service which commenced running to Queen's Cross in 1953.

A charming view of George Square in 1896 with a big sister showing her little brother one of the City's wonders — a new Corporation Horse Tram. The background Municipal Buildings seem to pale into insignificance by comparison!

A look up George Street from George Square shows the Royal Technical College. In 1948, when this photograph was taken, the "Tech" in the distance beyond the tram had yet to be extensively developed and receive university status as the University of Strathclyde.

Glasgow's most famous street, Sauchiehall Street, in 1910 had some development yet to take place. On the left of the "white" cars is the Copland and Lye building. To the right is The Picture House whose impressive facade has been retained in the development of the Savoy Centre.

Sauchiehall Street looking west from Renfield Street junction seems quiet in this 1920s scene. Bruce's furniture shop building was later well known as Lauder's Bar — meeting place for "resting" theatricals.

A look up Union Street towards Renfield Street illustrates the distinctive style of Forsyth's building. The Cadoro is on the immediate right and later formed part of the Reo Stakis empire.

Renfield Street in 1936 from Gordon Street corner. The "white" tram is heading for Mosspark — always believed to have the best trams although those allocated were often among the oldest in the fleet. On the right is Austin Reed's store. Up the hill is the Paramount (later Odeon) cinema.

The disappearance of the Grand Hotel has been mourned far more than anything else lost in demolition which anticipated the M8 Ring Road. This splendid view was taken in the 1880s before construction of Charing Cross Mansions which occupied the site on the extreme right.

A second look at the Grand Hotel cannot be resisted. A sprightly "white" tram blurs its way past the camera's time exposure. An inspector is waiting to check its time outside Mackinlay's schoolbook shop.

Glasgow's Mitchell Library is justifiably envied throughout the land. This building was opened in 1911 and many of the books were transferred from the earlier premises during one night by double deck tram.

The gentle curve of St George's Road from Charing Cross to Woodlands Road has gone together with its flanking shops. The M8 cut-and-cover has made this a windy, characterless waste despite the flowerbeds. Thankfully, the mansions to the rear remain.

TWO–WAY TRAMS

A procession of trams passes Central Station in 1954. This is the foot of Hope Street where a northbound tram to Anniesland pauses to let a Crookston-bound sister through. The variation in cleanliness between these two trams can be seen.

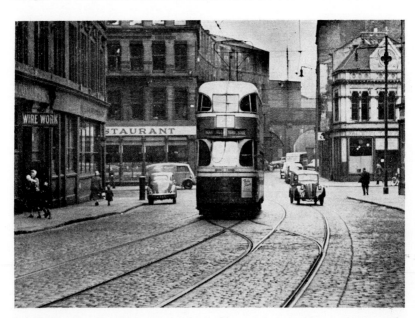

Moir Street was a loop for trams turning at Glasgow Cross amidst warehouses, pubs and railway arches. It is now part of a one-way traffic scheme and connects Gallowgate with London Road. This is 1954 and tram — No. 1010 — is one of those purchased from Liverpool a few months before.

How many family albums in Glasgow contain pictures like this? Here is one of highly polished tramcar No. 260 at Rouken Glen before the Great War. Conductor No. 1446 is Duncan McLean Drummond who joined the Tramways Department as a conductor at Newlands Depot. He died in February 1978 and his photograph found its way into this book.

TRAMS AND PARKS

Entrance to Rouken Glen.

The idea of the country park is thought to be new. But Glasgow had one in 1912 when this commercial postcard was bought. There were few houses near **Rouken** Glen at the time and the popular way to go there was, of course, by "red" tram.

Bellahouston Park was the venue for the 1938 Empire Exhibition. It was occupied by the militia during World War II and took some time to recover. The tram is heading into town between the White City Greyhound Stadium and the park.

This 1897 Botanic Gardens scene has been rescued from an old lantern slide. It was selected to show the odd station buildings of the Caledonian Railway and the mounted infantry passing by. The temporary loss of the restored Grosvenor Hotel in the terrace to the left makes it all the more poignant.

The monument at the tram terminus is to the Battle of Langside in 1568. The "yellow" tram's cross-over was later re-sited clear of the increasing traffic. Note the ornate horse-drawn hearse and the Queen's Park with less trees than it has now.

ARGYLE STREET

Gas lamps and horse drawn traffic were the order of the day in the 1880s when a photographer caught this scene from the then open bridge of the Central Station. Note the iron spiral ladder giving the only access to the open top deck of the horse trams.

It seems as if the viewfinder had frozen Argyle Street in mid-action. Precisely so as this is a frame from a very old cine film rescued just before disintegration and now reproduced for posterity. The date is 1901.

The building advertising Manfield's Boots to the right of the Coronation tram was one of Miss Cranston's Tea Rooms. This was her Dutch Tea Room and was complete with interior design by Charles Rennie Mackintosh. Opposite is one of Glasgow's disappearing clocks.

GREAT WESTERN ROAD

Great Western Road at Kelvinbridge is little changed except for the construction of a new Subway Station and some judicious restoration of the tenement property on the right: an area which has improved with time.

Great Western Road, Glasgow

Another look down Great Western Road to Botanic Gardens in the days when traffic was sparse enough to allow the tram wires to be suspended from centre poles. These were eventually replaced by the normal side poles although the track remained widely spaced.

Great Western Road is without doubt the finest approach into Glasgow and has seen much restoration of its quality buildings, including some of these in this 1936 view of Buckingham Terrace.

The photographer looks east along Great Western Road at Belhaven Terrace towards Kirklee. The Horse Tram can just be seen in the distance at its then terminus. Only the absence of mature trees, electric street lamps and motor traffic differentiate between then and now.

SUBURBAN CONTRASTS

Anniesland Station when it was called "Great Western Road" is shown here long before Kelvin Court and the unobtrusive Gartnavel General Hospital development. The Bank of Scotland building still exists.

Looking west towards Dunbartonshire under the railway bridge at Anniesland Station shows how the road was scooped out to afford enhanced clearance for top-covered trams. The photo was taken in 1954.

HYNDLAND ROAD, GLASGOW.

The well proportioned red sandstone tenements in Hyndland Road have stood the test of time. Here are two aspects of the same location at the top of Clarence Drive. Above is the early terminus of the "blue" service before it was diverted along Dumbarton Road. Below, looking from the opposite direction is a 1954 view illustrating little change over fifty years; a situation which has been maintained to this day.

BRIDGES

The canal bridge at Dalmuir, now removed, used to be the connection with the Dumbarton Tramways where you could board a tram for Balloch. No such luck in 1954 when this Standard Double Bogie tram regains terra firma with a series of staccato clicks over the rail joints.

It was this swing bridge at Kilbowie Road, Clydebank, located beside a low railway bridge which restricted service 20 to single deckers. These little trams rarely came near Glasgow's city centre and many of its citizens were totally ignorant of their existence.

Opened in 1927, George V Bridge provided plenty of transport interest. On the one hand there were the Clyde Steamers and the Burns & Laird Belfast ships while on the other the LMS trains crossed by their own bridge into the Central Station.

A southbound "blue" tram about to cross Jamaica Bridge at Broomielaw. Paisley's store on the left still thrives despite its location on the extreme edge of the City Centre and is little altered externally from this 1912 view.

Overleaf: In 1919 Jamaica Bridge was reported to be carrying 145 trams per hour — a figure which would be exceeded until the opening of George V Bridge could provide some relief. This view, however, dates from August 1936.

Standing as it did beside St George's Cross the Empress Theatre was far too distant from the city centre to enjoy popularity. Despite purchase by Jimmy Logan and some imaginative bookings, his re-named "Metropole" eventually closed and is dormant.

The Glasgow Empire was the premier variety theatre and its first house Monday night was generally admitted to be "death" for English comics. However, if Glasgow's discerning audiences loved them they could do no wrong. Jack Radcliffe, appearing then, would have been quite at home.

Here is Elmbank Street with the Beresford Hotel at the top and the King's Theatre to the left of the tram. This theatre was opened in 1904. It used to stage the "Half-Past-Eight" summer shows. Sold by Howard & Wyndham to Glasgow Corporation, The King's still thrives.

In 1955 "Half-Past-Eight" became "Five-Past-Eight" and, for that year only, was advertised on trams, like 834 seen here in Sauchiehall Street. The billing was (in order) "Jack Radcliffe, Jimmy Logan, Olga Gwynne, Kenneth McKeller". No trams actually passed the Alhambra where these shows were then produced.

CROSSES

Two contrasting views of Shawlands Cross: 1905 above and 1935 below. The gusset building still stands but the country houses behind in the upper view gave way to the Elephant Picture House shown below. But this has gone too. Now the arms of Kilmarnock and Pollokshaws Roads embrace a major shopping development.

HAWLANDS CROSS, GLASGOW.

Bridgeton Cross itself is still the heart of a redeveloping community. In 1910 this "yellow" tram is about to swing hard right towards Glasgow Green past the dentures manufacturer's signpost extolling "Teeth — fit and workmanship guaranteed, from 2/6d" (12½p).

It took some detective work to determine just where this was. Not only have the buildings come down, the junction is no longer there. Anderston Cross has been lost in the approaches to the Kingston Bridge and Clydeside Expressway.

SUBURBAN SCENES

CUMBERNAULD ROAD.

A "red" tram heads for Riddrie along Cumbernauld Road before the first World War, dropping passengers at Alexandra Park. This is not far from where a small boy cherished an ambition to have his address appear in print on a ticket as a tramway fare stage. His name was Jack House.

Alexandra Parade, and St. Andrews U. F. Church, GLASGOW.

It used to be said that if Glasgow were ever invaded from the East the enemy would never penetrate the congestion in Alexandra Parade! In 1910 there seemed to have been no problem. The dearth of traffic other than the omnipresent tram will be noted.

Glasgow's principal exhibition centre is the Kelvin Hall, burned down in 1925 and replaced by this building in 1927. This photograph was taken around 1934 from one of the high points of the Kelvingrove Art Galleries.

Dumbarton Road in Partick at its western edge in 1953 when the two railway bridges were still extant. Behind the camera there is now a gap where the Clydeside Expressway joins the northern approaches to the Clyde Tunnel.

Maryhill has seen much devastation in recent years in the name of progress. The building on the left, now demolished, was inscribed "Maryhill Cross". But this is 1906.

Bilsland Drive is the setting for a tram on one of Glasgow's circular services. It is about to cross Balmore Road without the aid of the present traffic lights. The flats behind have recently received extensive renovation and updating.

Springburn has been immortalised for many in the books by John Thomas and Molly Weir. It would be ungallant to suggest that Molly would remember Balgrayhill in 1910 but the scene changed little until well after the Second World War.

Much of Townhead has been razed and new houses built. Its former main artery, Parliamentary Road, has been eliminated and through traffic by-passes the area by a circuitous route. These trams were photographed on the 32 service in September 1954.

Nithsdale Road in Pollokshields was traversed by the "yellow" cars on the short route from Paisley Road Toll to Mount Florida. This was the last service within the city to be operated entirely by open-top trams. Little has changed here and Kitchin's Pharmacy still trades.

Trams would appear to have run past the Dixon Halls in Cathcart Road around 1906 without the use of overhead wires if this commercial postcard is to be believed. Presumably the retouching artists thought them unsightly and erased them!

The inevitable discussion at a tramway junction was when the crews argued as to who went first. No different at Mount Florida where a Paisley Road Toll-bound "12" meets a "13" for Milngavie. The trolleybus wires are already strung for the "13"s successors.

Victoria Road remains a thriving South Side shopping centre. Once home of the "yellow" trams, this scene was captured from the Queens Park gates looking towards Eglinton Toll. The time is the 1920s.

A bicycle ride on Glasgow's cobbled streets was just the thing if you had taken medicine and forgotten to shake the bottle. This cyclist seems set to beat the Standard Tramcar to the junction at Parkhead Cross in this 1953 view.

The State Cinema in Shettleston Road was just the kind of prey to succumb to the advancing craze for Bingo. While showing films like "The King and I" the crowds could still be pulled in.

The entrance to Parkhead Depot where an ex-Liverpool "Green Goddess" passes a sand wagon about to deliver its load from Admiral Street for Parkhead's complement of trams. These were almost the only cars in the works fleet regularly seen in daylight.

Govan Tram Depot at Lorne School was a busy place before and after peak hours with trams entering and returning from service. The forest of poles already planted in 1957 was an early warning of the conversion of the "7" and "12" tram services to trolleybuses in the following year.

An Ibrox bound "green" tram bears left at Paisley Road Toll before the Great War. The Ogg Brothers also owned Copland & Lye's department store. The Old Toll Bar still displays fine examples of etched pub glass in these days of plastic and laminated chipboard.

The tramcar on service "40" has just entered Paisley Road West from the extra-long siding at Ibrox terminus. In happier days this would be filled with special trams for Rangers' home matches. Latterly the only occupant would be an occasional "40".

TO MILNGAVIE

A "Coronation" tram bound from Milngavie to Clarkston thunders into Stockwell Street as it crosses Argyle Street. Stockwell Street was the home of the original Metropole Theatre, the China Bazaar and the railway bridge to St Enoch Station.

The demonstration track of the Bennie Railplane can be seen to the left of the tram in this 1956 Milngavie scene. The photographer did not have the weather on his side and vowed to return to better the attempt. When he did, the structure was being dismantled.

Rutherglen's Main Street in 1911. When the trams were withdrawn to within the Glasgow City Boundaries in 1956-57, those to Rutherglen and Burnside remained in operation.

Uddingston tram terminus was a meeting place between the Lanarkshire Tramways and those of Glasgow Corporation. There was no physical connection between the two here. The Tunnocks Tea Room sign prompts the question, how many of his red vans were there in 1933?

Cambuslang's Main Street with the photographer providing a diversion for the local people. Cambuslang was the meeting point with the Lanarkshire Tramways Company where the tracks **were** connected, although no interworking took place.

Coatbridge Main Street in 1931 when through traffic used this thoroughfare. The "green" tram in the background has come all the way from Paisley and beyond — a journey which would have cost only 2½d (1p).

TO RENFREW

This part of Renfrew Road near Hillington is particularly exposed and several trams were blown from their tracks over the years. The terminus just beyond the tram was formerly designated "Renfrew Aerodrome" but was re-titled "Hillington Rd" for security reasons during the 1939-45 hostilities.

Renfrew Cross in 1913 with two "blue" cars on the service to Keppochhill Road standing at the terminal stub. The tracks in the foreground belong to the Paisley District Tramways Company, taken over in 1923.

Mearns Road at Clarkston was one of the few terminal points with a facing cross-over. For a tram to park here today would cause chaos among indiscriminately-parked cars despite a one-way traffic scheme.

A view of Paisley's Municipal Buildings from the Cenotaph in 1957. The last tram ran in Paisley in May of that year. 146 in the foreground was the very last to cross the city boundary at Ralston before abandonment beyond Crookston Road.

A pleasant suburban view in Glenfield, Paisley, with a Coronation tram climbing to its terminus at the top of the hill. Although they went out of use in 1957 these tracks survived those in Glasgow by many years. The tram itself — 1274 — now resides at the Seashore Trolley Museum in Maine, U.S.A.

Barrhead is home of vitreous china and copper tubes — examples of which can be seen even in the Kremlin, some say. Here is the Main Street, much redeveloped since it was caught in time in 1956.

The private tram track at Darnley left the roadside at this point. Behind the Cunarder tramcar is Darnley Hospital and the tower of the since-demolished fire station. In front of the tram is a crossing for a mineral line.

With screens already set for the return journey, 474 pauses at the compulsory stop where Thornliebank's Main Street joins Rouken Glen Road. The houses to the rear have been demolished and a filling station occupies the site.

This little tram was the sole survivor from the electrified horse tram fleet. It used to operate a shuttle service in Finnieston Street. It is seen here ending its days at Abbotsinch where it was suited to the very light traffic on that country road. Because of this, the route was an early casualty, being replaced by Corporation buses in March 1933.

A 1956 night shot shows the very last tram leaving Crossstobs terminus north of Barrhead. The "14" tram was a convenient and cheap method of reaching the Glasgow shopping centres, one which has never been replaced.

Although Glasgow's last trams ran in triumphant procession on 4th September 1962, the Burgh of Clydebank could not be outdone and had her own last tram two days later. Coronation tram 1282 was chosen for this ceremony and was, coincidentally, selected by the S.T.M.S. for the Crich Tramway Museum collection.

AND FINALLY ...

For once the rules are broken and the tram is pictured rather than the scene — and it's not even Glasgow. This is 1282, the same tram which features overleaf as Clyde-bank's last. It has been rebuilt in the Crich Tramway Museum workshops in a quite remarkable restoration project. The photograph was taken in February 1978 during commissioning trials which preceded public running on the Museum's own demonstration tracks.

PHOTOGRAPHIC CREDITS

Photographs used in this book have come from the following sources and are gratefully acknowledged. The term "collection" has been used where there was no identification to enable full credit to be given.

T. & R. Annan & Sons Ltd: Cover, 8a, b, 9b, 23a, b, 24-5, 29b.

Ian M. Coonie: 26a, 35a, 36a, b, 37a, b, 39a, b.

Gavin Drummond collection: 7a, 13, 15a.

D. Frodsham: 48.

The "Glasgow Herald": 22b.

M. Morton Hunter collection: 16.

George Lane collection: 5b, 6a, 9a, 10b, 11a, b, 14a, 15b, 17b, 18b, 19a, 20a, 21a, 28a, b, 29a, 30a, b, 31a, 32a, 33a, 34a, b, 35b, 38a, 40a, 41a, b.

Kenneth F. Mackay: 43b, 44b, 45a, 47a.

Strathclyde Regional Archives: 12a.

Alastair Stirling: 47b.

S.T.M.S. collection: Frontispiece, 6b, 7b, 18a, 22a, 40b, 42b, 43a, 44a, 46.

A. A. Taylor collection: 5a, 10a, 19b.

T.M.S. archives: 17a.

R. J. S. Wiseman: 12b, 14b, 20b, 21b, 26b, 27a, b, 31b, 32b, 33b, 38b, 42a, 45b.

BLOCKS. Generous contributions towards the cost of blockmaking have been made by the following S.T.M.S. members:

Reg Barber 23b; David S. Brown 18a, 20a, b, 21a, 43a; Ian L. Cormack 41a; Brian T. Deans 21b; Wm Douglas 28b; John G. Fender 17b; Hugh Gilmour 38a; J. D. Gillies 45a; David Henderson D.Sc. 12a; Paul Hewett 35a; David Hunt 37b; Stuart M. Little 39b; Colin Lees 46; Brian M. Longworth 17a; Colin Morrison B.Sc. 31a; Charles Potter 37a, 47a; Tom Paterson 40a; Tom Quinn 47b; Alan Ramsay 18b; Author 48; Bill Tuckwell 15b; Geo. H. Williamson 31b; Geo. F. T. Waugh 8a.